A Down-Home Twelve Days of Christmas

By
Nancy Allen

Illustrated by
Apryl Stott

PELICAN PUBLISHING COMPANY
GRETNA 2017

*The word "Pelican" and the depiction of a pelican are
trademarks of Pelican Publishing Company, Inc., and are
registered in the U.S. Patent and Trademark Office.*

Library of Congress Cataloging-in-Publication Data

Names: Allen, Nancy, 1952- author.
Title: A down-home twelve days of Christmas / by Nancy Allen ; illustrations
   by Apryl Stott.
Description: Gretna, Louisiana : Publican Publishing, [2017]
Identifiers: LCCN 2016040559| ISBN 9781455622986 (hardcover : alk. paper) |
   ISBN 9781455622993 (e-book)
Subjects: LCSH: Christmas—Arkansas. | Arkansas—Humor. | Christmas—Humor.
Classification: LCC GT4986.A8 A55 2017 | DDC 394.266309767—dc23 LC record available at
https://lccn.loc.gov/2016040559

Printed in Malaysia
Published by Pelican Publishing Company, Inc.
1000 Burmaster Street, Gretna, Louisiana 70053

Lovingly, to a wise and funny woman, Barbara Sanders. —NA

To my girls. Hold out for your NASCAR driver. —AS

On the first day of Christmas . . .

On the first day of Christmas, my true love sent to me . . .

A possum in a sweet gum tree.

Dear Billy Ray,
   If you aren't the sweetest old thing! MeMaw had the best time shootin' that ol' possum out of that big old tree. Too bad she slipped on one of them gumballs. The break ain't that bad, in spite of all her hollerin', and the Doc says she might could get her cast off by Easter.
      Hugs and Kisses,
         Cyndi Lou

On the second day of Christmas, my true love sent to me . . .

Two armadillos and a possum in a sweet gum tree.

Dearest Billy Ray,

Why, you are just too good to be true! MeMaw has the best way to roast an armadillo you ever did eat, and we had one with all the fixin's. Yum! We couldn't cook up the other one. It got runned over.

Hugs and Kisses,
Cyndi Lou

On the third day of Christmas, my true love sent to me . . .

Three hunting dogs, two armadillos, and a possum in a sweet gum tree.

Dear Billy Ray,

Them dogs is just too cute. I'm guessing they's missing their mama, because they bay all night. I'm sorry about the armadillos. We just can't keep them out of the street. I don't know what I'm going to do with all them gumballs. We tried painting them red and hanging them on the Christmas tree, but they keep falling off, and then Memaw steps on them with her good foot.

Really, Billy Ray, we have enough. You can stop now.

Love, Cyndi Lou

On the fourth day of Christmas, my true love sent to me . . .

Four mockingbirds, three hunting dogs, two armadillos, and a possum in a sweet gum tree.

Billy Ray,

I just can't imagine what you think I'm going to do with four mockingbirds. You can't cook 'em. I'm having a heck of a time cleaning up after six dogs, all baying like fools after a bunch of hissing possums. And them armadillos! Six of them lying dead in the street with their little paws in the air. It's pitiful. At least I can use some of the gumballs to cover up their carcasses.

    -Cyndi Lou

On the fifth day of Christmas, my true love sent to me . . .

Five razorbacks, four mockingbirds, three hunting dogs, two armadillos, and a possum in a sweet gum tree.

Precious Billy Ray,

At last, a present we can use!
Memaw can't butcher them herself, what
with her cast and all. But I'm sure I
can figure out how to do the deed.
Just think--barbecue! But, Billy Ray,
this just won't do. We can't have
mockingbirds flying all over the house,
not to mention what else they do.
And all over the linoleum, too. The
dogs take up so much space in the
double-wide that I've had to set up
a tent in the yard, but the stink of
dead armadillo is about to drive me
insane. I think the neighbors have called
the sanitation department, and
Memaw's pretty put out.

                              Annoyed,
                              Cyndi Lou

On the sixth day of Christmas, my true love sent to me . . .

Six guys from the deer woods, five razorbacks, four mockingbirds, three hunting dogs, two armadillos, and a possum in a sweet gum tree.

Billy Ray,

NOW YOU JUST STOP! Have you EVER SMELLED a guy just out of the deer woods? And they didn't even bag a deer. Those old boys can't shoot! If they could, I'd have them take care of them hogs, rootin' and tearin' all over the block. All they do is drink beer and put the empties in the armadillos' paws. I can't sleep at night for all the hissin' and howlin' going on. The only safe place for me is up a tree, and the possums DON'T SHARE!

— C.L.

On the seventh day of Christmas, my true love sent to me . . .
Seven catfish swimming, six guys from the deer woods, five razorbacks, four mockingbirds, three hunting dogs, two armadillos, and a possum in a sweet gum tree.

You are just MORE trouble than I can pray over. I'll NEVER forgive you for putting me through a day of <u>hog</u> <u>butcherin'</u>! And the bathtub is full of catfish, so NOW I can't bathe them guys from the deer woods. (Did I tell you how much they STINK?) At least we can feed them, if I can get Memaw to take her Head OUT OF THE OVEN. DON'T even ask about the dogs.

On the eighth day of Christmas, my true love sent to me . . .
Eight Walmart shoppers, seven catfish swimming,
six guys from the deer woods, five razorbacks, four mockingbirds,
three hunting dogs, two armadillos, and a possum in a sweet gum tree.

IF YOU DON'T STOP NOW,
I'M GONNA GET MY COUSIN
LEROY TO BEAT YOU UP!
I mean it! Can you even guess
what them gals from Walmart
are getting up to with them
deer wood guys? ON MY
FRONT LAWN?

YOUR WORST
NIGHTMARE,
Cyndi Lou ¨

On the ninth day of Christmas, my true love sent to me . . .
Nine bluegrass pickers, eight Walmart shoppers, seven catfish swimming,
six guys from the deer woods, five razorbacks, four mockingbirds,
three hunting dogs, two armadillos, and a possum in a sweet gum tree.

Enclosed, you will find sixteen bills from Walmart, a citation from the Sanitation department, a veterinarian bill for spaying and neutering twenty-four dogs of varying ancestry, a bill for carpet cleaning (mockingbird damage), one doctor's bill, and a receipt from the Motel 6, where we have been driven to seek refuge from the noise of mandolins and Dobros, not to mention the cloggers who tagged along.

On the tenth day of Christmas, my true love sent to me . . .
Ten NASCAR racers, nine bluegrass pickers, eight Walmart shoppers, seven catfish swimming, six guys from the deer woods, five razorbacks, four mockingbirds, three hunting dogs, two armadillos, and a possum in a sweet gum tree.

Dear Billy Ray,

I fear it is only fair to tell you that Memaw has left us. She flew to Dallas yesterday with the sheriff's deputy sent to arrest us for disturbing the peace, and to take her to a sanitarium. He feels certain that the twitching won't set off the detectors at the airport, and the doctor says the panic attacks will stop with time.

I'm sending nine of the NASCAR racers to your house to drop off the nine remaining possums and most of the rest of the livestock. Twenty-eight dogs won't fit in those cars, so they'll just run along behind. That's all they're good for anyway, chasing cars.

In bitterness, Cyndi Lou

P.S. I'm keeping one of the racer guys.

On the eleventh day of Christmas, my true love sent to me . . .
Eleven Baptist preachers, ten NASCAR racers, nine bluegrass pickers, eight Walmart shoppers, seven catfish swimming, six guys from the deer woods, five razorbacks, four mockingbirds, three hunting dogs, two armadillos, and a possum in a sweet gum tree.

Dear Billy Ray,

   Bless your heart, the spiritual touch was just what I needed to get some perspective on this situation. The wedding was real nice, with plenty of good home cookin'. Them shopping gals really know how to put on a spread, and they can sew up a storm, too. I got me a real pretty wedding dress, and a ring too. The deer woods guys gave me away, and the bluegrass musicians played fiddle and banjo and all, and it was just lovely. We'll be driving to the Gulf for the honeymoon, so you won't be seeing me no more.

                              -Cyndi Lou

On the twelfth day of Christmas, my true love sent to me . . .
Twelve muzzle loaders, eleven Baptist preachers, ten NASCAR racers, nine bluegrass pickers, eight Walmart shoppers, seven catfish swimming, six guys from the deer woods, five razorbacks, four mockingbirds, three hunting dogs, two armadillos, and a possum in a sweet gum tree.

TO: Mr. Billy Ray Smith

FROM: Deputy Sheriff Dwayne Jones

RE: Memaw Brown

This letter is to inform you that Mrs. Edna Sue Brown, aka Memaw, has eluded my custody. She was last seen in the company of shoppers, racers, hunters, musicians, and assorted animals and was headed your way. She and her companions are armed and considered dangerous.

AUTHOR'S NOTE

The Twelve Days of Christmas was first published in England in 1780 as a rhyme and may have its origins in France. The tune we all know and sing comes from an arrangement of a traditional folk tune by English composer Frederic Austin. The song celebrates the twelve days following Christmas Day and ending on Twelfth Night, or Epiphany (January 6).

Countries all over the world have their own versions of the song, including New Zealand, France, Scotland, and the Faroe Islands. Surely my own region with its unique culture and history, wonderful and diverse people, and stunning natural environment should have its own variation. *A Down-Home Twelve Days of Christmas* is an homage to some funny and unmistakable aspects of Southern culture.